LEGENDARY GOALKEEPERS INSPIRING GREATNESS IN THE SOCCER FIELD

Kurt Dissel

All rights reserved. No part of this publication may be reproduced, distributed or transmitted in any form or by any means, including photocopying, recording, or other electronic or mechanical methods, without the prior written authorization of the publisher, except in the case of brief quotations embodied in critical reviews and certain other noncommercial uses permitted by copyright law. Under no circumstances will any blame or legal responsibility be held against the publisher, or author, for any damages, reparation, or monetary loss due to the information contain within this book, either directly or indirectly.

Legal Notice:

This book is copyright protected. It is only for personal use. You cannot amend, distribute, sell, use, quote or paraphrase any part, or the content within this book, without the consent of the author or publisher.

CONTENTS

INTRODUCTION i

GIANLUIGI BUFFON 7

Some Goalkeepers Curiosities 12

MARC-ANDRÉ TER STEGEN 14

Some Goalkeepers Curiosities 19

KEYLOR NAVAS 22

Some Goalkeepers Curiosities 27

THIBAUT CORTOIS 30

Some Goalkeepers Curiosities 35

CLAUDIO TAFFAREL 38

Some Goalkeepers Curiosities 43

UBALDO MATILDO FILLOL 46

Some Goalkeepers Curiosities 51

PETR ČECH 54

Some Goalkeepers Curiosities 59

IKER CASILLAS 61

Some Goalkeepers Curiosities 67

MANUEL NEUER 70

Some Soccer Curiosities 75

EDWIN VAN DER SAR 78

Some Soccer Curiosities 84

OLIVER KAHN 87

THE VAR 92

Goalkeeper in action 94

CONCLUSION 95

INTRODUCTION

In the enchanted world of soccer, where stories of victory are painted on the field and aspirations soar on the wings of goals scored, there is a position that represents toughness, discipline, and a never-ending drive to be the best: the goalkeeper. With every goal scored, dreams take flight and the field becomes a canvas for stories of victory. The fascinating stories of these goalkeeper heroes are told in this book, which not only celebrates their skill on the field but also looks into the huge effects they've had on life as a whole.

The Sound of Dreams

Picture yourself standing under the crossbar, the sound of soccer boots hitting the grass, and the ball flying towards you with all of your hopes and dreams on it. This is where the goal keeper lives. They protect dreams and keep hopes alive. Figuring out what it takes to be the best goalkeeper in soccer is the start of a journey that is full of qualities that go beyond the field. Young people who want to follow their own dreams can find strength in this journey.

Being Brave: Facing the Unknown

At the heart of being a goalkeeper is the need to be brave. To be the best goalkeeper, you need to do more than just stop powerful shots. You also need to be brave when facing the unknown with courageous heart. Kids learn how important it is to stand tall when things are unknown by seeing this bravery in real life. You learn to be brave on the soccer field, and you use that bravery in real life, whether you're trying something new, facing a fear, or standing up for what's right.

Precision: Getting Through Life's Challenges

The accuracy needed to see where a ball is going as it hurtles toward the goal mirrors to the precision needed to deal with life's challenges. With their great timing and ability to calculate, goalkeepers teach young dreamers to be careful about how they go about achieving their goals. Like a soccer game, life requires you to be very careful when making choices, having goals, and taking steps on purpose to reach them.

Resilience: your ability to bounce back stronger

The path of a player is full of missed saves, goals given up, and times when they lose. But what makes someone a real guardian of the goal is not failures but the strength to bounce back up stronger. Just like a journey, life is full of ups and downs. Young dreamers use the resilience they learn on the soccer field to help them find their way through life's obstacles. It teaches them that failures are not losses but chances to get better and stronger.

Remembering Your Roots: Being Humble

The most important thing for the best goalkeepers to have in the world of soccer stars is respect. When young people have big dreams, it's important for them to stay focused and remember where they come from. When someone is humble,

they can remember the values that their family, teachers, and the community that raised them taught them. It's a lighthouse that tells kids to learn from the past, value their starts, and appreciate the work that everyone does to move forward.

How to Learn from Legends

Not only the soccer field is a place where matches take place but also, it's a school where lessons from legends and role models are taught over and over again. In the same way that goalkeepers learn from what their predecessors did, young dreamers should learn from the stories of those who came before them. Young people who want to follow their dreams look up to the stars of the game and learn from their stories of perseverance, sportsmanship, and humility.

How Many Hours of Work

They spend a lot of time training, and it shows in every amazing save they make. Being a goalkeeper isn't all fun and games; it's also a lot of drills, routines, and repetitions. Young people with big dreams need to know that to be the best at anything, whether it's school, the arts, or sports, they have to be dedicated, practice, and be willing to put in the hours.

The Costs and Sacrifices

There are lots of things you have to give up to be a goalkeeper. You have to miss many things that you would love to be part on, and sacrifices that aren't just on the soccer field in order to get better. Similarly, following your dreams in life often means to do the same thing. It could mean giving up short-term pleasures for long-term goals, spending time learning new skills, or having to make tough decisions to stay true to one's goals.

Difficulties and Shortcomings

A goalkeeper's journey is not a smooth ride across a sunny field. There are many problems and issues with it that test the goalkeeper's skills. Conceding a goal, facing criticism, or dealing with injuries are part and parcel of this arduous path. Yet, it's in overcoming these difficulties that the goalkeeper discovers the strength within. In the same way, life is full of problems and failures. Young people with big dreams need to know that problems are not barriers, but chances to learn and grow. Accepting your flaws and learning from your mistakes are important parts of getting better.

How to Learn Values Through Sports

Why should kids think about sports as a way to learn moral values? Like life, the soccer field is a blank slate where values and traits like discipline, teamwork, resilience, and persistence are not only taught but also lived and experience first-hand. Sports become a metaphor for life and give kids a real-world, active way to learn essential life skills.

Now, why should kids think about becoming keepers? It's fun to make dramatic saves, but there are also lessons to be learned in life. Soccer is a mirror of the world because of how teams work and what each player is responsible for. This classroom is also a place where keepers learn morals that go beyond the soccer field.

Teamwork: Achieving Together

People don't score goals by themselves in soccer; teams work together to do it. The defenders, midfielders, and players help the goalkeeper do his job. In the same way, most of the time, reaching your life goals means working together with others. Young dreamers need to know how important it is to get along with others and know that working together can lead to bigger successes.

How to Learn from Defeats

There are times when goalkeepers face defeats, but that's when they learn and get better. In the same way, losses in life are not signs of failure but chances to grow. Kids need to be willing to take on challenges, learn from their mistakes, and see losses as opportunities to get better. Sport teaches the invaluable lesson that losses are not the end but a chapter in the larger narrative of success.

Building Character

The soccer field turns into a place where people can build character. Kids learn good character traits like honesty, sportsmanship, and respect for both teammates and opponents when they play sports. Individuals develop these traits beyond the game, making them responsible and respectful citizens. Kids learn how to deal with challenges in a gracious and humble way through sports.

In the end, the qualities needed to be the best goalkeeper in soccer are also the qualities that make individuals the best versions of themselves in life. Young dreamers put on their metaphorical "goalkeeper gloves" and step onto the canvas of life, ready to face the unknown, handle challenges with precision, bounce back stronger, embrace discipline, and persevere through the marathon of dreams. The soccer field is more than just a place to play. It's also a training ground where kids can learn how to play the big game of life, where they can become the guardian of their dreams.

Let's discover the stories of these eleven amazing goalkeepers and learn from them all the valuable lessons they have to share. The road is yours,

GIANLUIGI BUFFON

Gianluigi Buffon "Gigi"

Gianluigi Buffon was a young boy who lived in the beautiful Italian town of Carrara. He had dreams that were as big as the Tuscan hills. His path from the cobblestone streets of Carrara to the world's most famous soccer stadiums would become a story of resilience, triumph, and remembering where he came from.

He was known as Gigi, and his name was Gianluigi. He fell in love with soccer while playing silly games as a child in the dusty streets of Carrara. As Gigi's happiness grew, the soccer ball became her steady and constant companion. He became interested in goalkeeping all of a sudden when he saw his father, Adriano, taking care of the goalposts at local matches. Because he was interested, Gigi with a burst of curiosity, decided to follow in his father's footsteps.

But Gigi's path to fame was not easy. The rough soccer field he played on was different from the smooth venues he'd later play in. In the rush of challenges, there were some temporary goalposts, broken nets, and an old ball. Even though things were hard, Gigi was determined and faced them head-on. The cobblestone streets of Carrara were his test, his proving grounds, and he stepped up to every task with a burst of resilience.

Gigi joined the youth school of the Italian soccer club Parma when he was 13 years old. There were times when the transition from Carrara to a professional environment was both exciting and challenging. Gigi had to deal with challenges he had never dealt with before: tough competition, rigorous training, and times when he missed the comforting hug of the Tuscan hills.

As Gigi worked on his skills, his sudden brilliance became clear. He quickly moved up the ranks and played his first game in Serie A for Parma when he was 17. A lot of people were interested in the young keeper, but Gigi stayed grounded, like the Carrara marble that surrounded his home town.

Gigi took on even more challenges when he joined Juventus, one of the best teams in Italy. The spotlight was so bright that it hurt his eyes, and the pressure was so strong that it shook the arenas. But Gigi started to feel calm quickly, and that would become his trademark. He went into every match with ease and confidence.

Gigi played for Italy in the 2006 FIFA World Cup, which was a big turn of events in his life. The final game against France was a rush of excitement that kept everyone on the edge of their seats. Italy won the World Cup as Gigi made some amazing saves in the penalty shootout. It was a burst of pride an iconic moment that could be heard through the hills of Carrara when he lifted the trophy.

Off the field, Gigi's heart was just as big as his accomplishments. His outburst of kindness went to many good causes, especially those that helped kids and the environment initiatives. Gigi understood that being successful wasn't just about what he did for himself, but also about giving back to the community that helped him reach his goals and ultimately nurtured his dreams.

As Gigi's work reached new heights, he never forgot the helpful boost that sent him on his way. His family, his coaches, and the town of Carrara were always there for him as constant anchors. Gigi often went back to his roots out of gratitude, where he inspired the next generation of soccer fans with his presence and words of support. Gigi was known for his charity work. In addition to his other charitable endeavors, after every match he auctioned off his personalized captain's armband for charity. In 2012, Buffon joined the "Respect Diversity" Programme, through UEFA, which aimed to fight against racist, discrimination and intolerance in soccer. On September 1, 2014, Buffon, along with many current and former soccer stars, took part in the Match for Peace which was played at Rome's Stadio Olimpico, with the proceeds being donated to charity. In October 2019, Buffon was named a UN Goodwill Ambassador for the World Food Programme.

After a great career, Gigi returned to Juventus in 2018. Fans all over the world were thrilled to see him again. Even though he was famous, he still went into every match with the same fire and passion that drove him in his early days in Carrara.

That's how the story of Gianluigi Buffon, the goalkeeper whose heart was as big as the Tuscan scenery, spread to kids all over the world becoming a source of inspiration. From the cobblestone streets to the big venues and stadiums, his journey showed how important it is to keep going, work hard, and stay true to your roots. Young people could learn from Gigi's story that if they worked hard at their dreams, no matter how strange they seemed, they could come true.

He was highly regarded as one of the greatest goalkeepers of all time, he is one of the few recorded players to have made over 1,100 professional career appearances and holds the record for the most appearances in the Series A. On August 2, 2023, Gianluigi Buffon at the age of 45 and after a 28-year playing career, he announced his retirement from professional soccer. After retiring from professional soccer, Buffon was appointed by the FIGC as the head of delegation of the Italy National Team on August 5, 2023, a position last held by the late Gianluca Vialli.

Some Goalkeepers Curiosities

Claudio Taffarel:

Claudio, the Brazilian goalkeeper, once played in a match with a broken hand, showcasing his dedication to the game.

Jose Luis Chilavert:

Chilavert, from Paraguay, was not only a fantastic goalkeeper but also scored an impressive number of goals during his career, primarily through free-kicks and penalties.

Manuel Neuer:

He once went 1,147 minutes without conceding a goal in Bundesliga, setting a new record.

Davide Egea:

Egea, a rising star, gained fame for his incredible reflexes and shot-stopping abilities at a very young age.

Peter Schmeichel:

Schmeichel, a Danish legend, captained his national team to their first major international trophy, the UEFA Euro 1992.

Diago Costa:

Costa is known for his acrobatic saves and quick reactions, earning him the nickname "The Octopus."

Yassine Bounou:

Bounou, from Morocco, played a crucial role in Sevilla's UEFA Europa League triumphs with exceptional saves during penalty shootouts.

Emi Martinez:

Martinez, an Argentine goalkeeper, had a remarkable journey from being Arsenal's backup to becoming the hero for Aston Villa in the Premier League.

Gianluigi Donnarumma:

Donnarumma made his professional debut for AC Milan at the age of 16, quickly becoming one of the youngest starting goalkeepers in Serie A history.

Mike Maignan:

Maignan, a French goalkeeper, earned his place in the national team with consistent performances, showcasing his composure under pressure.

MARC-ANDRÉ TER STEGEN

"Guardian of the Net: Marc-André Ter Stegen"

A young boy named Marc-André Ter Stegen fell in love with soccer in a cute German town called Monchengladbach where the sound of balls moving through the narrow streets could be heard everywhere. Marc-André's Road to becoming a famous goalkeeper began when he was born into a family that loved soccer as much as they loved family dinners.

Marc-André learned how to play soccer for the first time not in a fancy venue but on the patchy grass of a nearby park with his brother at the age of 2. He started kicking the ball playing in his family backyard. A loose group of kids from the neighborhood got together for makeshift games because they all wanted to be like their heroes. They had no idea that one of them would become the net's guardian: a young boy with lightning-fast reactions and a never-ending desire to win.

The way to success, on the other hand, is often full of problems. The first problem Marc-André had was that area youth teams didn't pick him because he was too short. But, as with all great stories, our hero didn't let being turned down break his heart. Instead, he used it to push himself to do better and show that size didn't matter when you were determined.

Marc-André didn't give up and worked on his skills in the dusty backyard of his family house. Because he saw how passionate his son was, his father became his first teacher and taught him how to play keeper. As Marc-André worked hard to get better at keeping goal, the hours changed into days and the days into years.

At the age of 4, his grandfather enrolled him into the Borussia Monchengladbach's academy. When he first began playing soccer, he was a striker as he loved to score goals. Getting into a youth academy gave him access to better tools and structured training. It was an important event that would change the life of a young boy with big hopes. At the age of 10 and after his manager's humiliating comments about his running style that forced him into changing his position on the field giving him an ultimatum to leave the club or to stay as a permanent goalkeeper, something he agreed upon afterwards.

There were some hard times in life at the school. Marc-André had to compete with other goalkeeper-to-best who were all trying to get the prized starting spot. But our hero stood out because he was determined and worked hard. He got to be in between the posts not just because he was good, but also because he worked hard, was determined, and was always trying to get better. Ter Stegen rose through the academy ranks with ease and when he turned 16, he was promoted to Monchengladbach's senior side and this marked the beginning of his professional career. But Ter Stegen spent the entire of his youth career at his hometown's club academy. He progressed through the academy ranks and had a very successful amateur career with Monchengladbach's B team. After three seasons as Gladbach's starter, Ter Stegen was picked up by the FC

Barcelona Club for €12 million in the summer of 2014 as the Catalans looked to replace long serving goalkeeper Victor Valdes.

When Marc-André got a call from FC Barcelona, one of the best football clubs in the world, it was the turning point in his career. His journey began with the move to the Catalan giants. It will be full of challenges at the top level of the sport. It was a huge responsibility for Marc-André to defend the goal for a club like Barcelona, but he took it on with the same energy that he showed when he was younger.

At Barcelona, success did not happen quickly. Marc-André had to deal with doubters, close scrutiny, and the difficult job of replacing a legendary goalkeeper. Still, with each amazing save and calm pass of the ball, he put the naysayers to rest. His play not only made him Barcelona's first choice, but it also won him friends all over the world.

Even though Marc-André played in La Liga and the Champions League, he never forgot where he came from. He stayed involved with his hometown by helping local initiatives and inspiring the next generation of goalkeepers. His story gave young people who want to be talented hope and showed them that with dedication and hard work, any dream is possible, no matter how crazy it seems. Finally, kids, Marc-André Ter Stegen's story shows us that size and running style doesn't matter if you have the drive and don't give up. Our hero's trip from the dusty fields of a small German town to the grandeur of Camp Nou shows that any dream is possible if you have the right mindset.

Remember Marc-André's story as you put on your boots. Take on the obstacles, enjoy the wins, and never forget where your dreams came from. Because, like Marc-André Ter Stegen, you could become the goalkeeper and the hero of your own soccer story.

Some Goalkeepers Curiosities

Bernd Leno:

Leno, the German shot-stopper, is known for his precise distribution, often initiating quick counter-attacks with accurate throws.

Andre Onana:

Onana, from Cameroon, started his career as an outfield player before transitioning to become one of the most promising goalkeepers in Europe.

Ederson:

Ederson, the Brazilian goalkeeper, is famous for his exceptional ball-playing skills and accurate long-range passes.

Marc-Andre Ter Stegen:

Ter Stegen, the German goalkeeper, is renowned for his incredible footwork, making him a crucial part of Barcelona's possession-based style of play.

Gianluigi Buffon:

Buffon, an Italian legend, is the oldest goalkeeper to win the UEFA Champions League, achieving this feat with Juventus in 2021.

Thibaut Courtois:

Courtois, the Belgian goalkeeper, is exceptionally tall, standing at 6 feet 6 inches, making him a formidable presence in the goal.

Iker Casillas:

Casillas, a Spanish icon, started his youth career as a striker before his coach noticed his goalkeeping potential.

Edwin Van der Sar:

Van der Sar, from the Netherlands, holds the record for the longest unbeaten streak in Premier League history, lasting 1,311 minutes.

Higuita:

René Higuita, the Colombian goalkeeper, is famous for popularizing the "scorpion kick" save during a match against England.

Fillol:

Ubaldo Fillol, an Argentine goalkeeper, won the Golden Ball for the best player in the 1978 FIFA World Cup, a rare feat for a goalkeeper.

Dino Zoff:

Zoff, an Italian legend, became the oldest player to win the FIFA World Cup at the age of 40 in 1982.

KEYLOR NAVAS

KEILOR ANTONIO NAVAS "KEYLOR NAVAS"

A young boy named Keylor Navas lived in the beautiful town of Perez Zeledon in Costa Rica. The waves lapping at the shore and the sun painting the sky with warm colours were his home. His dreams were as endless as the lush jungles that surrounded him. He had no idea that his path from the dusty fields of Perez Zeledon to the famous soccer stadiums of the world would be one of hard work, perseverance, and a strong bond with the places that helped him grow his goals.

He loved soccer so much that it felt like a warm breeze in his heart. He learned how to play on the dusty fields of Perez Zeledon with the ball, which made him happy. Keylor first became interested in goalkeeping after seeing his neighbourhood heroes make amazing saves that seemed to defy gravity as well as followed his goalkeeper idol's Léster Morgan. It was like a mission for Keylor; the job was a natural gift that would shape his future.

Still, Keylor had to go through a lot of tough situations to become one of Costa Rica's best keepers. The soccer fields he played on were rougher than the well-kept areas he would later watch over. Keylor was raised in a low-income family in San Isidro de El General, a town in the Southeast of San José and everything for him and his family was a huge effort. The economical situation of Keylor's family plus his lack of height were some of the struggles he had to deal with on his early beginnings. But Keylor, on the other hand, had a strong will, strong motivation and an immense faith on God and turned every problem into a spurt of motivation.

Keylor played his first game as a professional for Saprissa, a club in the Costa Rican league, when he was 18 years old. Being able to play professionally for the first time after playing in the dusty fields of Perez Zeledon was both exciting and hard. Keylor was thin and not tall enough, which made people doubt him, but his lightning-fast reflexes and unwavering focus put them to rest. Keylor showed off his unique skill by standing tall between the goalposts with a burst of determination.

Keylor played for Costa Rica in the 2010 FIFA World Cup, which was a big turn of events in his life. The event brought out a lot of feelings in the Costa Rican people, and Keylor's great goalkeeping was a big part of their amazing run to the quarterfinals. The people of Perez Zeledon were so proud that it could be heard in the mountains and rivers. Just before the FIFA World Cup in 2010, Keylor signed for Albacete Balompié of the second division in Spain and he started his soccer career on different teams in Europe from then on.

Away from the game, Keylor's heart was as warm as his home country. His act of kindness went beyond the soccer field. Keylor was involved in a lot of community projects, especially ones that helped young people grow and sports programs for poor kids. He knew that success wasn't just about what he did for himself, but also about giving back to the community that had helped him become the person he was.

Keylor played for a number of teams, including Levante in Spain and, finally, Real Madrid. Every new chapter brought a new set of problems and chances. In 2014, Keylor was a key part of Costa Rica's successful return to the World Cup, which was another stroke of fate. It was impossible to describe how happy Perez Zeledon was, and Keylor's play got him a move to Paris Saint-Germain, one of the biggest clubs in the world.

Some sports experts think Navas is one of the best keepers in the world, and others think he is the best in CONCACAF history. Navas is an energetic keeper who is best known for his speed, agility, and athleticism in goal, as well as his quick reflexes and ability to stop shots, which help him make up for his lack of height. He has also gotten praise from the media for how well he played in important games and how often he made tough, important saves for his team in crucial situations. Manuel Almunia, a former keeper, praised Navas in 2017 and called him "the prototype model" keeper. He also said, "He's spectacular between the posts; he's brave, skilled, and very agile." He keeps his focus, and he's also highly clever... I think he deserves all the praise he gets for what he's done.

Even though Keylor faced some problems and setbacks along the way, his heart never gave up. In 2018, he became the first goalkeeper to win three straight UEFA Champions League titles with Real Madrid. This showed that hard work and persistence can make dreams come true.

When Keylor got to the top of his field, he never forgot the boost of support that helped him get there. His family, his teachers, and the dusty fields of Perez Zeledon were always there for him. Keylor often went back to his roots out of gratitude, where he inspired the next generation of soccer fans with his appearance and words of support.

So, kids all over the world found hope in the story of Keylor Navas, the keeper whose heart was as strong as the jungles of Costa Rica. From the dusty fields to the big arenas, his journey showed how important it is to keep going, work hard, and stay true to your roots. Keylor's life showed young people that if they worked hard at their dreams, no matter how strange they seemed, they could come true.

Some Goalkeepers Curiosities

Oliver Kahn:

Kahn, a German goalkeeper, is known for his intense and commanding presence on the field, earning him the nickname "Der Titan."

Petr Cech:

Cech, the Czech goalkeeper, holds the record for the cleanest sheets in Premier League history.

Claudio Bravo:

Bravo, the Chilean goalkeeper, is known for his quick reflexes and exceptional penalty-saving skills, making him a reliable choice in crucial moments.

Kasper Schmeichel:

Kasper, following in his father Peter Schmeichel's footsteps, played a pivotal role in Leicester City's historic Premier League title win in the 2015-2016 season.

Alisson Becker:

Alisson, the Brazilian goalkeeper, is not only known for his shot-stopping prowess but also for scoring a stunning header for Liverpool in a Premier League match.

Keylor Navas:

Navas once trained as a bullfighter during his youth, showcasing his courage and determination even outside the football field.

Emiliano Buendía:

Buendía, primarily an outfield player, started his career as a goalkeeper before transitioning to become an attacking midfielder.

Alphonse Areola:

Areola, a French goalkeeper, has a unique ritual of touching the goalposts before every match for good luck.

Bernd Leno:

Leno is known for his charitable work, actively supporting various causes, and establishing the Bernd Leno Family Foundation.

Yann Sommer:

Sommer, the Swiss goalkeeper, is an avid piano player, showcasing his talents beyond the football pitch.

Pepe Reina:

Reina, a Spanish goalkeeper, is a well-known guitar enthusiast and often plays for his teammates during team gatherings.

THIBAUT CORTOIS

THIBAUT CORTOIS, THE GIRAFFE

Thibaut Courtois was a young boy from Bree, Belgium. He had hopes as big as the Belgian waffles he enjoyed on lazy Sunday mornings when he didn't have to do anything. Little did he know that his journey into the world of soccer would be a captivating tale of perseverance, triumph, and never forgetting where you come from.

In the narrow streets of Bree, Thibaut's life started with soccer. It was more than just a game; it was a way of life. Thibaut and other kids would practice their soccer skills in makeshift games with the soccer ball, which would make a joyful sound as it bounced along the cobblestone roads. He became interested in goalkeeping even though he was playing volleyball all the time with his parents and his bigger sister in their backyard. Thibaut was born to be a volleyball player not a soccer player. As a young boy, he was clumsy and absent minded at a times. Even accidents were very common at his early age, it was never dull but at the age of five he decided to play soccer.

Although Thibaut was 18 months younger that his teammates, he looked strong and powerful, he was a robust kid. But it wasn't easy for him to get to the top of the world. Thibaut was put through a series of tests and continuous rotations that showed how determined he was. Being tall between the goalposts, he understood that his peers didn't understand why he was tall, which was supposed to help him. His size made them laugh, calling him the "The Giraffe," but Thibaut, with a burst of strength, loved it.

He didn't have to wait long for the scouts of Racing Genk, a local first division team to notice his skill. He was eight years old when they asked him to come to one of their training session days. Soon after he joined the Genk, a small team in the Belgian Pro League, which was his first real club. For the young goalkeeper, the trip from Bree to Genk was like a sudden vacation. Thibaut had a hard time with things like juggling school and soccer and long trips on Belgium's twisting roads. But each problem was a puzzle that had to be solved, a chance to show that dreams could come true with dedication and hard work. During summer times, Thibaut kept playing volleyball teaming up with his sister Valerie and his dad, but at that point he was still playing as a left back for Genk's youth team. Under the nines tournaments his coach decided to put him between the posts, where he really excelled and adjudged as the best goalkeeper but his parents didn't want him to be pin down on one fixe position.

Scouts took notice of Thibaut's sudden rise in skill, and soon he was playing goal for the powerful Chelsea FC in the English Premier League in July 2011. There was a lot of excitement during the change, but the problems got worse. It was hard for the young goalkeeper because of how fast the game was going, the fact that they didn't speak the same language, and the rainy English weather. Still, Thibaut got through the storm with a burst of drive.

Thibaut's fate changed quickly in 2014 when he went on loan to Atletico Madrid for the next three seasons. The sun kissed his skin in Spain, and the soccer gods were happy for him. Atletico Madrid made it to the UEFA Champions League final thanks to Thibaut's amazing saves and strong presence in goal. The world was amazed as the young goalkeeper beat all odds and became a role model for other young athletes who want to follow in his footsteps.

Thibaut didn't forget the things that helped him grow, even when he was successful. He went back to Chelsea with a lot of new knowledge and a thankful heart and became their first- choice goalkeeper. Thibaut Courtois, the boy from Bree, was a great player all over the world, but he stayed as grounded as the cobblestones in his city.

Thibaut loved more than just soccer when he wasn't playing. His sudden act of kindness went to good causes, especially those that helped kids follow their dreams. Thibaut knew how powerful dreams could be, and he wanted to help people who needed it.

Thibaut reached another important goal in 2018 when he joined Real Madrid, which is every football player's dream. Bree was filled with excitement as people celebrated the rise of their hometown hero to one of the most famous clubs in the world. As the season went on, Thibaut kept shining, making amazing saves in La Liga and the UEFA Champions League.

As Thibaut rose to the top, he never forgot the boost that helped him get there. He always loved his family, his teachers, and the town of Bree. Thibaut often went back to his roots with a sense of humility, inspiring the next generation of soccer fans with his appearance and words of support. He is involved in various charitable activities. He is an ambassador for the NGO's Save the Children and has also worked with the Belgian charity "Kom of tegen Kanker", which supports cancer patients.

To this end, children all over the world looked up to the story of Thibaut Courtois, the kind giant with lots of dreams. From the small streets of Bree to the big stadiums of Europe, his story showed how important it is to keep going, work hard, and stay true to your roots. Young people could learn from Thibaut's life that if they worked hard at their goals, they could make any dream come true, no matter how strange it seemed.

Some Goalkeepers Curiosities

Edouard Mendy:

Mendy, the Senegalese goalkeeper, initially worked as a delivery truck driver while pursuing his soccer dreams in France.

Alireza Beiranvand:

Beiranvand, an Iranian goalkeeper, used to work as a shepherd, honing his goalkeeping skills in the fields before making it to professional soccer.

Hugo Lloris:

Lloris, the French goalkeeper, is fluent in English and Spanish, showcasing his linguistic talents beyond his soccer skills.

Petr Cech:

Cech is an accomplished drummer and has even played in a band, showcasing his musical talents off the pitch.

Walter Zenga:

Zenga, an Italian goalkeeper, had a brief acting career and appeared in an Italian movie titled "Quando eravamo repressi."

Thibaut Courtois:

Courtois has a keen interest in basketball and even considered pursuing a career in the sport before dedicating himself to soccer.

Manuel Neuer:

Neuer is a certified pilot, showcasing his passion for flying planes in addition to his goalkeeping skills.

Salvatore Sirigu:

Sirigu, an Italian goalkeeper, is an avid fan of art and has a collection of paintings, showcasing his appreciation for creativity.

Víctor Valdés:

Valdés, a former Barcelona goalkeeper, transitioned to become a successful football coach after retiring from professional play.

Rui Patrício:

Patrício, the Portuguese goalkeeper, once saved four penalties in a single shootout during the UEFA European Championship, earning his team a spot in the final.

Dida:

Dida, the Brazilian goalkeeper, is known for his superstitions, including wearing the same pair of gloves for important matches.

CLAUDIO TAFFAREL

CLAUDIO TAFFAREL

A young boy named Claudio André Taffarel lived in the sunny city of Santa Rosa, Brazil, where the joyful beat of samba filled the air. His dreams were as big as the Amazon jungle. He had no idea that his path from the dusty streets of Santa Rosa to the biggest soccer stages in the world would become a story of hard work, determination, and a strong bond with the places that helped him grow his dreams.

His love for soccer was like a bunch of circus drums going off in his heart. The ball, which made him happy, was always with him when he played with his friends on the makeshift fields that were all over Santa Rosa. What got Claudio interested in goalkeeping after seeing his hometown hero, Emerson Leão, proudly put on the gloves. Claudio felt like the job was a calling, a natural urge that would shape his future.

But Claudio had to go through a lot of tough times to become one of Brazil's best goalkeepers. The rough soccer fields he played on were different from the well-kept fields he would later watch over. Claudio didn't have a lot of money, and the idea of getting good soccer gear seemed like a faraway thunderclap. Claudio, on the other hand, had a strong will and turned every problem into a spurt of motivation.

Claudio's first professional game was for Internacional, a club in the Brazilian league, when he was 18 years old. When he went from playing in the dirty streets of Santa Rosa to playing on a professional stage, it was both exciting and hard. People didn't trust Claudio because he was skinny and seemed to lack knowledge. But his exceptional performances soon caught the attention of scouts, and Claudio, on the other hand, stood tall between the goalposts and showed off his unique skill of making amazing saves and reading the game perfectly.

When Claudio played for Brazil in the FIFA World Cup in 1994, a series of events happened that would change his life. The event made the Brazilian people feel a lot of different things, and Claudio's great goalkeeping was a big part of their run to the final. The final game against Italy was very exciting, and Claudio's important saves in the spot shootout gave Brazil the win. Santa Rosa was filled with a rush of joy that was as bright as the colors of Carnival.

Claudio played for a number of teams, such as Parma in Italy and Galatasaray in Turkey. Every new chapter brought a new set of problems and chances. Another twist of fate happened in 2002, when Claudio was a key part of Brazil's World Cup victory. The final game against Germany was very emotional, and Claudio's steady play in goal helped Brazil win the title. The people of Santa Rosa were so proud that it could be heard all the way through the Amazon jungle.

Taffarel played 101 times for the Selecão, which makes him Brazil's most-capped keeper of all time and one of only a few players in world football history to have earned at least 100 caps for their country. When he retired in 2003, coach Carlos Alberto Parreira offered to set up a farewell game, but the player said he wasn't interested in all the fuss. He did, however, come back to play with Romário against Mexico in late 2004 to celebrate the 1994 World Cup win at the Los Angeles Memorial Coliseum.

Taffarel and Paulo Roberto, who used to play for Atlético Mineiro together, started a player agency that usually works with young players who have a lot of potential.

During the 1998 World Cup, the Brazil National Team trained at Trois-Sapins field in Ozoir-la-Ferrière, a suburb southeast of Paris. The mayor of the town suggested that the stadium be renamed after him.

When Taffarel returned to Galatasaray in 2004 as goalkeeper coach, he worked with old teammate Gheorghe Hagi. He returned to the club for the 2011–12 season, this time with Fatih Terim as manager. Before he left the Turkish team in 2019, Taffarel was short-term boss for two times.

He is a goalkeeper coach for both Liverpool (since 2021) and the Brazil national team (since 2014).

When Claudio got to the top of his field, he never forgot the boost of support that helped him get there. His family, his teachers, and the dirty streets of Santa Rosa were always there for him. With a sense of thanks, Claudio often went back to his roots, where he inspired the next generation of soccer fans by being there and saying nice things.

Even though Claudio faced some problems and hurdles along the way, his spirit never gave up. When he came back to Brazil after successful stays in Europe, he felt like he was going home. While working as a coach, Claudio continued to help Brazilian soccer by teaching young keepers who looked up to him what he knew.

Away from the field, Claudio's heart was really warm. His acts of kindness went beyond the soccer field. Claudio was very involved in community projects, especially those that helped young people grow and sports programs for kids who didn't have much. He knew that success wasn't just about what he did for himself or what he had achieved, but also about giving back to the community that had helped him become the person he was.

So, the story of Claudio Taffarel, the goalkeeper whose heart beat as fast as the samba became an inspiration for kids all over the world. From the dirty streets to the big stadiums, his story showed how important it is to keep going, work hard, and stay true to your roots. Claudio's life showed young people that if they worked hard at their dreams, no matter how hard they seemed, they could come true. Let it remind you that talent and hard work are a powerful combination, and when you want something very hard, no obstacle is big enough to overcome.

Some Goalkeepers Curiosities

Ali Gabr:

Gabr, an Egyptian goalkeeper, is also a talented artist, often showcasing his drawings and paintings on social media.

Samir Handanović:

Handanović, the Slovenian goalkeeper, has a degree in economics, highlighting his academic achievements alongside his soccer career.

Jan Oblak:

Oblak, the Slovenian goalkeeper, is an accomplished chess player, showcasing his strategic thinking beyond the soccer field.

Jean-Marc Bosman:

Bosman, a former Belgian goalkeeper, is famous for the "Bosman ruling," a landmark legal case that changed soccer transfer regulations.

Rinat Dasaev:

Dasaev, a Soviet and Russian goalkeeper, won the Golden Foot Legend Award in 2018, recognizing his outstanding career and contributions to the sport.

Sepp Maier:

Maier, a German goalkeeper, is known for his unique training regimen, which included catching chickens to improve his reflexes.

Gordon Banks:

Banks, the English goalkeeper, achieved legendary status for his famous save against Pelé in the 1970 World Cup, known as the "Save of the Century."

Lev Yashin:

Yashin, the Soviet goalkeeper, remains the only goalkeeper to ever win the Ballon d'Or, awarded in 1963 for his exceptional performances.

David De Gea:

De Gea, the Spanish goalkeeper, worked as a supermarket employee before joining Atletico Madrid's youth academy, showcasing his humble beginnings.

Faryd Mondragón:

Mondragón, a Colombian goalkeeper, became the oldest player to appear in a FIFA World Cup match, playing at the age of 43 in the 2014 tournament.

Jordan Pickford:

Pickford, the English goalkeeper, has a distinctive ritual of touching the crossbar and goalposts before each game for good luck.

UBALDO MATILDO FILLOL

UBALDO MATILDO FILLOL, THE DUCK FILLOL

An Argentine boy named Ubaldo Matildo Fillol lived in the wide streets of San Miguel del Monte, where the sound of tango danced through the air like a passionate explosion. He had dreams as big as the Argentine pampas. He went from the dusty fields of San Miguel del Monte to the most famous soccer arenas in the world. It was a story of hard work, perseverance, and never forgetting the roots that helped him grow his dreams.

I love Ubaldo, who is also known as "El Pato" (The Duck). He discovered his love for soccer while playing games with his friends as a child in the sunny streets of San Miguel del Monte. He played with his friends until the sun went down, and the ball, which made him happy, became his best friend. Ubaldo became interested in goalkeeping all of a sudden at a neighbourhood game, where he offered to stand between the goalposts. However, he had his own idol since he was a child and that one was Agustín Mario Cejas. This goalkeeper was his unavoidable reference like it was Amadeo Carrizo sometime after. He felt like the job was like a second skin—it was a natural calling that would shape his future.

But Ubaldo had to go through a lot of tough situations to become one of Argentina's best goalkeepers. He had to help out his father before he was able to go to school. After school he used to play soccer until the night. But he only had one pair of shoes and really had to take care of them as there was no money for more. On many matches he had to play barefoot, the main thing was to play no matter how. They were not fixed positions but all the time the goalkeeper was missing, he was the one who took over. But Ubaldo, who had a strong will, used every problem as a chance to get even more motivated.

When Ubaldo was 17, he played his first game for Quilmes youth division, a club in the Argentine league. But a year later when he was 18 years old, he played in the First division (the Argentine top division) playing for Quilmes vs Huracan on May 1,1969. Up from playing in the dusty streets of San Miguel del Monte to the big stage as a professional was both an exciting and difficult change. People didn't trust Ubaldo because he dressed in an unusual way and had long hair that ran like a spark of rebellion. Ubaldo, on the other hand, stood tall between the goalposts and showed off his unique skill agility and quick reflexes that allowed him to make acrobatic saves.

In 1974, Ubaldo played for Argentina in the FIFA World Cup, as part of the roster, which was a big turning point in his life. The game made the Argentine people feel a lot of different things, and Ubaldo's great goalkeeping was a big part of their run to the final. Argentina lost the championship game, but Ubaldo's great play won him the title of Best Goalkeeper of the Tournament, which made a lot of people happy all over the pampas.

In Ubaldo's career, he played for many teams, such as River Plate and Racing Club. Playing for Racing Club, Ubaldo met his all-time mentor Angel Labruna, who dedicated a lot of time on Ubaldo's constant training, development and learning. Every new chapter brought a new set of problems and chances. In 1978, Ubaldo was a key part of Argentina's victory at the FIFA World Cup, which was another stroke of fate. The final game against the Netherlands was very exciting, and Ubaldo's great saves made sure that Argentina won. When Ubaldo lifted the World Cup trophy, the Argentine pampas erupted in joy. It was a moment of glory that made soccer history and cemented his place in it.

When Ubaldo reached the top of his field, he never forgot the boost of support that helped him get there. The sun-drenched fields of San Miguel del Monte, his family, and his teachers were always there for him. With a sense of thanks, Ubaldo often went back to his roots, where he inspired the next generation of soccer fans by being there and saying nice things.

Off the field, Ubaldo's heart matched the passion of his performances. His acts of kindness extended beyond the soccer field. Ubaldo actively participated in community initiatives, got involved in different projects particularly those supporting underprivileged children. He used his influence to make a positive impact on the lives of others and understood that success was not just about personal accomplishments.

Along his journey, Ubaldo faced many problems and controversies, but his spirit never gave up. It filled him with pride and memories to play for Argentinos Juniors again, the team where he began his professional career. Ubaldo played well into his 40s, showing that age wasn't important when you were passionate about something.

After that, kids all over the world looked up to the story of Ubaldo Matildo Fillol, the keeper whose heart was as big as the Argentine pampas. From the sunny streets to the big venues, his journey showed how important it is to keep going, work hard, and stay true to your roots. Young people learned from Ubaldo's life that if they worked hard at their dreams, no matter how hard they seemed, they could come true.

Some Goalkeepers Curiosities

Tim Howard:

Howard, a former U.S. national team goalkeeper, once held the record for the most saves in a single World Cup match, making 16 saves against Belgium in 2014.

Rogerio Ceni:

Ceni, a Brazilian goalkeeper, is the highest-scoring goalkeeper in soccer history, with over 130 goals, primarily from free-kicks and penalties.

Igor Akinfeev:

Akinfeev, the Russian goalkeeper, captained the national team to a historic quarter-final appearance in the 2018 World Cup, showcasing his leadership skills.

Eduardo Galeano:

Galeano, a Uruguayan journalist, wrote a famous passage called "Goalkeeper," paying tribute to the solitary and often underappreciated role of goalkeepers in soccer.

Djalma Santos:

Santos, a Brazilian right-back, was known for occasionally stepping in as a goalkeeper during matches, showcasing his versatility.

Fabien Barthez:

Barthez, a French goalkeeper, won both the FIFA World Cup and UEFA Euro in 1998, showcasing his dominance on the international stage.

Jens Lehmann:

Lehmann, a German goalkeeper, once saved two penalties in a shootout during the UEFA Champions League final in 2005, helping Arsenal secure the title.

Gianluigi Buffon:

Gianluigi Buffon has a remarkable record of saving penalties, showcasing his incredible shot-stopping abilities under pressure.

Claudio Taffarel:

He is known for his exceptional penalty-saving skills, making him a hero in shootout situations.

Victor Valdés:

Valdés has a vineyard in Spain, showcasing his passion for winemaking outside of his soccer career.

Jorge Campos:

Campos, a Mexican goalkeeper, was known for his colorful and extravagant jersey designs, showcasing his unique sense of style.

PETR ČECH

PETR ČECH, THE GUARDIAN OF DREAMS

In the beautiful town of Plzeň in the middle of the Czech Republic, there was a boy named Petr Čech who was born as a triplet along with his sister and a brother and who fell in love with ice hockey and soccer but the equipment cost forced him to play the significantly cheaper sport of soccer even though his preferred sport as a child was ice hockey. It would become his lifelong passion. His love for football would take him from the muddy grounds of his youth to the big stages of European football.

There was a small patch of grass where Petr's journey started. The sound of laughter mixed with the thud of a ball being kicked. The kids in the neighbourhood played soccer without any rules. Their dreams were as big as the sky. Petr stepped up to be the goalkeeper. He wore gloves that were too big for his hands and had a lot of drive. It would become his safe place, where he felt a link with the game that he couldn't put his finger on.

But it's never easy to become a sports star. Early on, Petr had problems, and some coaches weren't sure if he was ready to be a goalkeeper. He wasn't discouraged, so he used the doubters as fuel for his fire, turning their criticism into drive. They had no idea that they were taking on a future hero.

When Petr's family saw the spark in him, they became his biggest fans. Even though they didn't have much money, they scraped together every penny to buy him the gear he needed. They never let their limited means get in the way of his goals. That unflinching support became the base on which Petr's goals were built.

As a teen, Petr joined the youth school of Viktoria Plzeň, the club that he grew up with. Even though the training was tough, Petr's hard work and natural skill started to show. The dirty fields of Plzeň were now where a future star trained.

It all changed when Petr caught the attention of scouts from Sparta Prague, which is one of the best teams in the Czech Republic. He started a new chapter in his life when he moved to Sparta. This new chapter would see him rise through the ranks and become a top goalkeeper.

But the way to the top is never a straight line. In a match against Reading at the Madejski Stadium on October 14, 2006, a huge setback in the form of a major head injury put Petr's determination to the test. Many people didn't think he could get better, but after a head surgery, Petr overcame the problems with a drive as strong as the Vltava River. He went back out on the field to play and to change what it meant to be a goalkeeper.

Petr made his comeback in a Premier League match in a 2-0 defeat against Liverpool on January 20, 2007, wearing a rugby style headguard, something he continued to wear for the rest of his career.

On the European stage, Petr's skills were seen by many. Chelsea, a huge team in English sports, came calling. Moving to the Premier League, Petr made history in football by becoming a team captain. Petr became famous all over the world, not just in Plzeň, thanks to his success at Chelsea, where he won league titles and the Champions League.

Even with all the flare and stylish, Petr stayed grounded. He would never forget the dirty fields of Plzeň or how his family gave up things so he could follow his dreams. He was humble in interviews and public events, and emphasizing the values of hard work and persistence had shaped his life.

Petr was a great example for young keepers all over the world because he was strong both on and off the field. His story showed kids that they could achieve any dream, no matter how crazy it seemed, if they worked hard and didn't give up. Petr's story wasn't a fairy tale; it showed how important it is to keep going even when things get hard.

Remember Petr Čech's story as you put on your soccer shoes and head out to the field. You should paint your dreams on the muddy fields of your youth, and every failure should be seen as a way to get better. You can become the guardian of your own dreams and the star of your own sports story, just like Petr did.

On January 2019, Petr announced via an open letter on Twitter that he would retire from soccer at the end of the season and on May 29 of that year, he made the final appearance of his career in Arsenal's 4-1 defeat to his former club Chelsea in the 2019 UEFA Europe League Final. Nowadays Petr plays ice hockey as a goaltender for the Belfast Giants on loan from Oxford City Stars. In the 2023 off season, Petr played for the Elite Ice Hockey League defending champions, Belfast Giants, in a charity match to support the continuation of ice hockey in Ukraine amid the Russo-Ukrainian war.

Some Goalkeepers Curiosities

Júlio César:

César, a Brazilian goalkeeper, played a crucial role in helping Inter Milan win the UEFA Champions League in 2010, earning him widespread acclaim.

Dida:

Dida once played a crucial role in AC Milan's defense during the team's successful run in the early 2000s, showcasing his leadership skills.

Marcos:

Marcos, a Brazilian goalkeeper, played a key role in Brazil's World Cup triumph in 2002, earning him the nickname "Saint Marcos."

Javier Zanetti:

Zanetti, an Argentine right-back, played alongside many legendary goalkeepers throughout his career, providing a unique perspective on their skills.

Fernando Muslera:

Muslera, the Uruguayan goalkeeper, is known for his consistent performances and has been a mainstay for Galatasaray in the Turkish Super Ligue.

José Luis Félix Chilavert:

Chilavert was not only a skilled goalkeeper but also a vocal leader, often taking free-kicks and penalties, showcasing his confidence on the pitch.

Sebastián Saja:

Saja, an Argentine goalkeeper, once scored a goal from his own penalty area, showcasing his powerful and accurate goal kicks.

Loris Karius:

Karius, a German goalkeeper, played for Liverpool in the UEFA Champions League final in 2018, an event marked by an unfortunate mistake, showcasing the mental challenges goalkeepers face.

Brad Friedel:

Friedel, a retired American goalkeeper, had a lengthy career in the Premier League, showcasing his durability and longevity in top-level soccer.

Keylor Navas:

He holds the record for the most saves in a single UEFA Champions League season.

IKER CASILLAS

IKER CASILLAS, SAN IKER

In the lively town of Móstoles, Spain, there lived a young boy named Iker Casillas whose journey to the top of the soccer world was as remarkable as a thrilling match under the Spanish sun. He would go and revolutionise the term of modern goalkeeping.

Iker's story began on the dusty fields of Móstoles, near Madrid where the soccer ball was a burst of joy that danced between friends. Even as a young kid, Iker's fascination with goalkeeping was evident. His friends, amused by his acrobatics and dives, would often burst into laughter, unknowingly witnessing the early chapters of a soccer legend. As a very young kid, his father always took him to the Santiago Bernabéu to see Real Madrid playing vs. Athletic de Bilbao or Real Sociedad. Iker always knew he could play there one day.

Growing up in a modest neighborhood, Iker faced challenges that added a burst of difficulty to his dreams. The soccer field he played on was more of a patchwork quilt, a mosaic of dirt and patches of grass. Yet, instead of letting these shortcomings deter him, Iker embraced them as opportunities. With makeshift goalposts and weathered soccer balls, he honed his skills, turning the humble field into a canvas of dreams.

As Iker's passion for goalkeeping blossomed, his family stood as a pillar of support. However, financial difficulties cast a shadow over their unwavering belief. The burst of challenges threatened to sideline his aspirations, but Iker, with a heart brimming with determination, found a way. His family's sacrifices fueled his commitment to succeed.

Iker's talent didn't go unnoticed, and soon he found himself donning the colors of CD Móstoles, the local soccer club. His burst of talent shone brightly, but the road to glory was far from smooth. Financial struggles persisted, and the odds were stacked against him. Nevertheless, Iker, with a burst of resilience, continued to chase his dreams. Iker also played in Real Madrid's youth system knows as La Fábrica during the 1990 to 1991 season. On 1997 at the age of 16 and still a junior, he was called up to the senior team squad in the UEFA Champions League. After one season with the fourth-level C-team, where they won their regional group, he was in the running to be the club's first-choice goalkeeper.

In 1999, a burst of destiny unfolded when Iker made his debut for the Real Madrid senior team at the tender age of 18. The Santiago Bernabéu Stadium erupted in cheers as they witnessed the emergence of a star goalkeeper. Yet, the journey to the top was a rollercoaster of highs and lows.

Iker faced scrutiny and doubters, but his burst of resilience saw him through. With every challenge, he responded with spectacular saves and an unbroken spirit. His perseverance painted the canvas of his career with strokes of triumph.

The pinnacle of Iker's career came in 2010 when he captained the Spanish national team to victory in the FIFA World Cup.

The final against the Netherlands was a burst of intensity, and Iker's crucial saves earned Spain their first-ever World Cup title. His iconic moment, lifting the trophy amidst a burst of confetti, etched his name in soccer history.

Off the field, Iker's heart matched the grandeur of his achievements. He engaged in numerous charitable endeavors, a burst of kindness that touched lives beyond the soccer pitch. His commitment to helping others showcased a different facet of the legendary goalkeeper – a man whose influence reached far beyond the confines of a stadium.

Iker's career saw numerous triumphs, including five La Liga titles, three UEFA Champions League titles, and two UEFA European Championships with Spain. His impressive resume wasn't just a list of accomplishments; it was a testament to the impact one could have with a burst of talent, hard work, and a heart inclined towards others. Throughout the season playing for Porto and after finished in second place, his suffered an acute myocardial infarction that cut short his season.

As the final chapter of his playing career unfolded, Iker remained connected to his roots. He returned to FC Porto, a nod to the beginnings that shaped him. On August 4, 2020, Iker officially announced his retirement from professional soccer something that brought a burst of nostalgia on all his followers, a reflection on the journey from the dusty fields of Móstoles to the grand stages of world soccer.

And so, the story of Iker Casillas, a goalkeeper whose career mirrored a captivating novel, became a source of inspiration for generations. His life, both on and off the field, emphasized the importance of perseverance, hard work, and giving back. In the vibrant tapestry of soccer history, Iker's legacy stood as a shining example of how one person's burst of dreams could reverberate across the world, leaving an indelible mark for years to come. Iker never forgot his roots and all the people that supported him to make his dreams come true. In 2011, Casillas was named a Goodwill Ambassador for the Millennium Development Goals of the UN Development Program. In 2013, a street in the Móstoles municipality of Madrid was renamed Avenida de Iker Casillas in his honour. Iker also runs his own charity, The Fundación Iker Casillas. In 2018, he went to Moscow for the international social Football for Friendship meeting among other things that he has contributed.

In honour of his amazing saves, Casillas is often called "San Iker" or "Saint Iker." Many people think he is one of the best keepers of all time. He is famous for being very athletic, having quick movements, and being able to stop shots very well.

As you read about Iker Casillas's journey, let it motivate you to keep going after your dreams. Remember that where you're going and how hard you're ready to work to get there are more important than where you came from. The story of Iker shows that even the biggest dreams can come true with determination, hard work, and a "never give up" approach.

Remember the boy from Mostoles who could make amazing saves, kids? If you want to follow your own dreams, let Iker Casillas's story inspire you. You can do great things too if you are passionate, learn to work in a group, never be afraid to fight for them, protect, respect each other and believe that anything is possible as long as you truly love what you do in life. And as Iker said all the time to achieve fame, it is a great thing. It is amazing that people remember the goalkeeper and what he has done in the soccer field but most importantly people should remember the person and who the person really is, that is what is most remarkable.

Some Goalkeepers Curiosities

In the history of soccer, Latin America has had a number of great goalkeepers who set great examples for other players. These are some of the best keepers in the area:

Gilmar dos Santos Neves:

Gilmar played a crucial role in Brazil's success during the 1958 and 1962 World Cups, earning two consecutive titles.

Dino Zoff:

Zoff, born in Argentina but later representing Italy, is considered one of the greatest goalkeepers of all time. He won the 1982 World Cup with Italy.

Hugo Gatti:

Gatti, known as "El Loco," had a distinguished career in South American football, playing for clubs like Boca Juniors and River Plate.

Ubaldo Fillol:

Fillol was a key part of Argentina's national team during the 1978 World Cup, which they won on home soil.

Claudio Taffarel:

Taffarel played a crucial role in Brazil's 1994 World Cup triumph and had a successful career playing in Europe.

Rogério Ceni:

Ceni, a goalkeeper known for his goal-scoring ability as well, spent his entire career at São Paulo FC and is considered one of the best goalkeepers in Brazilian history.

José Luis Chilavert:

Chilavert was not only an outstanding goalkeeper but also one of the best goal-scoring keepers in history. He played for clubs like Vélez Sársfield.

Raul Navarro:

Navarro was part of the Uruguay national team that won the 1950 World Cup, and he played for clubs like Nacional.

Carlos Roa:

Roa gained fame during the 1998 World Cup with Argentina, where he helped his team reach the quarterfinals.

Keylor Navas:

While not traditionally part of South America, Navas has made a significant impact. He played a crucial role in Costa Rica's historic run to the quarterfinals in the 2014 World Cup and has had success with clubs like Real Madrid and Paris Saint-Germain.

These goalkeepers changed the past of soccer in Latin America and are remembered for their contributions to the game

MANUEL NEUER

MANUEL NEUER, "THE SWEEPER-KEEPER"

A young boy named Manuel Neuer had dreams as big as the Ruhr Valley. He lived in the middle of Gelsenkirchen, Germany, where the sounds of coal mines and soccer fields mixed. He had no idea that his path from Gelsenkirchen's playgrounds to the world's biggest soccer stadiums would be one of determination, toughness, and a strong bond to the places that helped him grow his goals. Like many other soccer players, such as Mesut Ozil, he attended to Gesamtschule Berger Feld. When he was two years old, he got his first soccer ball and. his first game was on March 3, 1991, 24 days before he turned five.

Manuel loved soccer so much that it gave him a lot of energy. The ball, which made him happy, was always with him when he played with his friends on the rough fields that were all over Gelsenkirchen. When Manuel saw the famous Oliver Kahn take charge of the German goal, he became instantly interested in goalkeeping even though his true hero was fellow German and former Schalke goalkeeper Jens Lehmann. Manuel felt like the job was a calling, a natural skill that would shape his future.

But Manuel had to go through a lot of tough situations to become one of Germany's best goalkeepers. The rough soccer fields he played on were different from the smooth fields he'd later protect. Manuel family didn't have a lot of money, and the dream of becoming one of the best German goalkeepers was very far away and difficult to project. Though

Manuel faced many problems, he was determined and used each one as a spur to get things done.

Manuel played his first game for Schalke 04, a club in the Bundesliga, when he was 20 years old. There were both thrills and difficulties when they went from playing on the rough fields of Gelsenkirchen to the professional stage. People didn't believe in Manuel because he was young, but his amazing shot-stopping skills and calmness under pressure put them to rest. Manuel showed off his unique skill by standing tall between the goalposts with a burst of determination.

In 2010, Manuel's life took an unexpected turn when he played for Germany in the FIFA World Cup. The event made Germans feel a lot of different things, and Manuel's great goalkeeping was a big part of Germany's run to the semifinals. The people of Gelsenkirchen were so proud that it could be heard in the coal towns.

Manuel worked his way up to play for Bayern Munich, which is one of the best teams in the world. Every new chapter brought a new set of problems and chances. In 2013, another lucky turn of events happened when Manuel was a key part of Bayern Munich's famous treble-winning season, which won the Bundesliga, the DFB-Pokal, and the UEFA Champions League. There was an unimaginable amount of happiness in Gelsenkirchen, and Manuel was praised as one of the best keepers in the world for his work.

Off the field, Manuel had the same kind of heart as the people in his hometown. His acts of kindness went beyond the soccer field. Manuel was very involved in community projects, especially those that helped young people grow and sports programs for kids who were not that fortunate. Being successful meant more than just what he did for himself. It also meant giving back to the people who had helped him become the person he was today.

When Manuel got to the top of his field, he never forgot the boost of support that helped him get there. His family, his teachers, and the rough fields of Gelsenkirchen were always there for him. Manuel often went back to his roots out of gratitude, where he inspired the next generation of soccer fans with his appearance and words of support. Neuer is a Catholic and supports a Catholic social action group in Gelsenkirchen that works to end child poverty as well as an Amigos-run youth club in Gelsenkirchen. Neuer set up a charity for kids and called it the Manuel Neuer Kids Foundation. His win of €500,000 for charity in a star version of the German show Wer wird Millionar? in November 2011 was a big deal.

Even though Manuel faced some problems and hurdles along the way, his spirit never gave up. He was very important to Germany's win at the 2014 World Cup. The Ruhr Valley was filled with a loud roar of joy that could be heard as far away as the coal mines. After Germany had been eliminated from the FIFA World Cup in Qatar in December 2022 at the group stage and will all the frustration and negative vibes still going in his head, and in order to clear his head, Manuel went skiing with a group of friends in the Alps to the south of Munich, where he got into a serious accident that kept him out of the session until October 28, 2023 Manuel played for the first time in 350 days in a match which ended in a 8-0 victory over Darmstadt. A month later, he extended his contract with Bayern Munich until June 30, 2025.

So, the story of Manuel Neuer, the goalkeeper whose heart was as strong as the German spirit, became an example for kids all over the world. From the dirty fields to the big arenas, his journey showed how important it is to keep going, work hard, and stay true to your roots. Young people could learn from Manuel's life that if they worked hard, if they push, really persist and chase at their dreams, no matter how hard they seemed, they could come true.

Some Soccer Curiosities

Soccer Ball Origins:

The first soccer balls were made of inflated pig bladders covered in leather, giving a whole new meaning to the term "pigskin."

Most Goals in a Match:

The highest-scoring soccer match recorded was a 149-0 victory by AS Adema against SO l'Emyrne in Madagascar in 2002. SO l'Emyrne intentionally scored own goals in protest.

The Largest Soccer Tournament:

The FIFA World Cup is the most-watched and widely followed sporting event globally, attracting billions of viewers. The tournament has been held every four years since 1930, except during World War II.

Laws of the Game:

The Laws of the Game, established by the International Football Association Board (IFAB), were first codified in 1863. They've evolved over time but remain the foundation of soccer rules worldwide.

Yellow and Red Cards:

The introduction of yellow and red cards as a means of disciplining players came about after English referee Ken Aston was inspired by traffic signals while stuck in traffic.

Offside Rule Evolution:

The offside rule has evolved significantly. In the early days, a player was offside only if they were ahead of the ball and the opponent's goal. The modern interpretation is more complex, considering the player's position and involvement in the play.

The Golden Goal:

The "golden goal" rule was briefly implemented in soccer, meaning the first team to score in extra time would win. It was used in major tournaments but was later abandoned.

Panenka Penalty:

The "Panenka" penalty, named after Czechoslovakian player Antonín Panenka, involves a cheeky and daring chip shot straight down the middle during a penalty shootout.

Own Goal Records:

The most own goals scored by a team in a single soccer match is three, a dubious record shared by Inter Milan and Las Palmas.

Innovative Corner Flag:

In the 1978 World Cup, the corner flags were made of fiberglass to prevent players from using them as weapons during heated moments.

Longest Soccer Match:

The longest recorded soccer match lasted for 36 hours and was played in Scotland in 2017. It was a charity match that raised funds for cancer research.

Soccer in Antarctica:

Soccer has been played in every continent, including Antarctica. Research station residents engage in friendly matches to stay active and maintain camaraderie.

EDWIN VAN DER SAR

EDWIN VAN DER SAR

A young boy named Edwin Van der Sar lived in the Dutch town of Voorhout, where the tulips sway in the wind like a surge of colour. His dreams were big as the fields that were around his house. He had no idea that his journey from the small town to the big sports stadiums of the world would become a story of hard work, determination, and the unwavering support of his family and friends.

Edwin fell in love with soccer on the cute streets of Voorhout. Edwin and his friends were playing soccer, which made the cobblestone roads ring with the sound of happiness. As quickly as lightning, Edwin became interested in goalkeeping when he learned that being the last line of defence was both a duty and an art form.

From the neighbourhood squares to the professional pitches, his trip was like a sudden adventure. Many things were hard for Edwin, but his tall body was the most confusing. His limbs moved on their own, and he was taller than most kids his age. His sudden surge of energy often caused him to dive and fall awkwardly, which made his friends laugh. But Edwin, who had a strong will, used his flaws to fuel his drive.

He attended the youth academy of Ajax, one of the best soccer clubs in the world, when he was 15 years old. From playing soccer in the neighbourhood to Ajax's tough training sessions, there were both lots of fun and lots of obstacles. It was hard for Edwin to deal with the sudden competition, the fast-paced professional training, and the times when he missed the tulip-covered fields of Voorhout.

As Edwin worked on his skills, his sudden brilliance became clear. He moved up quickly and played his first game for Ajax when he was 20 years old. When the young goalkeeper saw the big arenas and heard the roar of the crowd, he felt thrilled. But success came with its own problems and shortcomings.

Edwin was very important to Ajax's win in the UEFA Champions League in 1995. The final game against AC Milan was very exciting, and Edwin's important saves helped Ajax win the title. That day, the tulips in Voorhout stood a little taller, proud of the burst of brilliance their neighbourhood hero had shown on the big stage.

Edwin played for many teams, such as Fulham and Manchester United in the English Premier League. Every new chapter brought a new set of problems and chances. Another lucky turn of events happened in 2008 when Edwin made important stops in the penalty shootout against Chelsea to help Manchester United win the UEFA Champions League.

Edwin had a big heart that met the great things he had done. His act of kindness went beyond the soccer field. Edwin was very involved in good causes, especially those that helped kids' health and education. He knew that being successful wasn't just about what you did for yourself, but also about how you helped other people.

When Edwin got to the top of his field, he never forgot the boost of support that helped him get there. His family, his teachers, and the Voorhout fields covered in tulips were always there for him. With a sense of thanks, Edwin often went back to his roots, where he inspired the next generation of soccer fans by being there and helping out kids. A praise song for Van der Sar was played at the Amsterdam Arena on August 3, 2011. Wayne Rooney, John Heitinga, Louis Saha, Rio Ferdinand, Ryan Giggs, Paul Scholes, Nemanja Vidić, André Ooijer, Dirk Kuyt, Gary Neville, Michael Carrick, Edgar Davids, Giovanni van Bronckhorst, Boudewijn Zenden, and Dennis Bergkamp were on the "dream team" of the keepers. Alex Ferguson was in charge of the team. They played the first team for Ajax at the time, which was led by Frank de Boer.

Before this match, there were two shorter ones. Two games were played between young teams from Ajax and Manchester United. The first was between Ajax's 1995 team and the Netherlands' national team in 1998. Finidi George, Nwankwo Kanu, Frank de Boer, Winston Bogarde, Nordin Wooter, Ronald de Boer, Danny Blind, Patrick Kluivert, Marc Overmars, and Frank Rijkaard were all on the Ajax team, which was led by Louis van Gaal. Guus Hiddink was in charge of the Netherlands team, which had Wim Jonk, Dennis Bergkamp, Roy Makaay, Ruud Hesp, Aron Winter, Richard Witschge, and Pierre van Hooijdonk, among others.

Two million people watched it at its peak in the Netherlands alone, giving it a 26% share of the entire market. Because the match made so much money, Van der Sar announced afterward that he would be starting his own charity to help spend the money. The money from the match was supposed to go to the Make a Wish Foundation and Laureus.

Van der Sar played in the Soccer Aid 2012 Match on May 27, 2012, for the Rest of the World team in the first half. He stopped John Bishop from scoring from all the way across the field. An Irish comic named Patrick Kielty took his place at halftime. He also played in the Soccer Aid 2014 match on June 8, 2014, this time for the Rest of the World team in the first half. At halftime, Patrick Kielty came on and took his place.

Edwin stopped playing professional soccer in 2011 after a great career. He was filled with so much feeling as he said goodbye to the stadiums that had seen his amazing journey. That being said, Edwin's love for the game did not end when he retired.

After he retired, Edwin did a number of things connected to soccer, such as coaching and management. People who wanted to follow in his ways looked to his sudden wealth of knowledge and experience as a guide. It was Edwin's life that showed that dreams, no matter how hard they seemed, could come true with persistence, hard work, and keeping true to one's roots.

So, kids all over the world were moved by the story of Edwin Van der Sar, the goalkeeper whose heart was as big as the tulip fields in Voorhout. From the cobblestone streets to the big stadiums, his journey showed how strong desire can be and how important it is to never forget where you came from.

Edwin's life showed young people that if they worked hard at their dreams, no matter how hard they seemed, they could come true.

Some Soccer Curiosities

Goalkeeper's Glove Innovation:

Goalkeeper gloves have come a long way since their invention. Originally, keepers would use bare hands or leather gloves. Modern gloves feature latex foam for better grip and protection.

First Soccer Game on Television:

The first soccer match broadcasted on television was a friendly between Arsenal and Arsenal Reserves on September 16, 1937.

Goalkeeper Kit Evolution:

Goalkeeper kits have evolved from basic attire to colorful and distinct designs. The flamboyant choices often reflect a goalkeeper's personality on the field.

Penalty Spot Distance:

The penalty spot is precisely 11 meters (12 yards) from the goal line, a distance established in 1866 and maintained ever since.

Soccer as a Diplomatic Tool:

Soccer has been used as a diplomatic tool. During the Cold War, matches between the Eastern Bloc and the West were used to ease tensions.

Fastest Goal in Soccer History:

The fastest goal ever scored in professional soccer occurred just 2.8 seconds into a match. The goal was netted by Ricardo Olivera in 1998.

Soccer and the Space Race:

The Apollo 11 astronauts took a soccer ball with them to the moon, and a game was played during their mission.

Goal Line Technology:

Goal-line technology, introduced to determine whether the ball has crossed the goal line, uses cameras and sensors to provide instant and accurate decisions.

Substitution Rules:

Initially, substitutions were not allowed in soccer. The first substitution in an international match occurred in 1954, but it took until 1965 for substitutions to be allowed in domestic soccer.

Goalkeeper Communication:

Goalkeepers often use unique communication methods with their defenders, including specific hand signals or codes to convey instructions during a match.

The Oldest Soccer Club:

The oldest soccer club in the world is Sheffield FC, founded in 1857 in England.

OLIVER KAHN

OLIVER ROLF KAHN, THE TITAN

A young boy named Oliver Kahn had huge dreams. He lived in the middle of Karlsruhe, Germany, where the Black Forest echoed with stories of dreams that were as old as time. He had no idea that his trip from the poor streets of Karlsruhe to the bright stadiums of world soccer would become a story of determination, strength, and a strong bond with the places that helped him grow his dreams.

Oliver's passion for soccer was like a thunderbolt in his heart. The ball was always with him when he played with his friends in the muddy fields near his house. One of Oliver's first memories of being interested in goalkeeping was seeing the great Sepp Maier guard the German goal during the 1974 World Cup. Oliver felt like soccer was calling him, to be a goalkeeper was for him, a natural urge that would shape his future.

But Oliver had to go through a lot of tough situations to become one of Germany's best keepers. The soccer fields he played on were rougher than the well-kept fields he'd later protect. Oliver didn't have a lot of money, and he was very aggressive something that didn't help much on his inspirations. On the other hand, Oliver's strong will turned every challenge into a boost of drive.

Oliver played his first professional game for Karlsruher SC, a club in the German Bundesliga, when he was 18 years old. He started playing as an outfield player before becoming a goalkeeper. As soon as he moved from playing in the muddy fields of Karlsruhe to the competitive stage, he felt both excited and challenged. But people didn't trust Oliver because he was fiery and seemed to lack knowledge. Despite that, Oliver showed his unique skill for acrobatic saves and steady focus by standing tall between the goalposts with a surge of strength and energy. Later on, he got transferred to the Bayern Munich where he played until the end of his career with a commanding presence and aggressive style that earned him the nickname The Titan.

Oliver played for Germany in the FIFA World Cup in 1994, which was a big moment in his life. The event made Germans feel a lot of different things, and Oliver's great goalkeeping was a big part of Germany's run to the final. Oliver's play won him praise as one of the best goalkeepers of the tournament, even though Germany lost the championship game. This praise echoed through the Black Forest.

Oliver won his first German title with Bayern Munich in the 1996–97 Bundesliga season. The team won the German League Cup. Oliver was also named The German goalkeeper of the year for the second time in his career, the first time being in 1994.

Oliver played for a number of teams, such as Karlsruher SC and Bayern Munich. Every new chapter brought a new set of problems and chances. In 2001, Oliver led Germany to the

UEFA Champions League final with Bayern Munich, which was another stroke of luck. Oliver's leadership and drive won him praise on the biggest stage of European soccer, even though they had to deal with heartbreak.

Oliver played for the German national team from 1994 to 2006. After Andreas Kopke retired, he took over as starter, but he didn't play in the team that won the UEFA European Championship in 1996. Even though Germany wasn't one of the favourites to win the 2002 FIFA World Cup, Oliver's skill in goal helped them make it to the final, where they lost 0–2 to Brazil. Even though Oliver made a mistake on Brazil's first goal, he still won the Golden Ball as the tournament's best player.

Oliver's heart was as honest as the people in his neighbourhood. He was kind to people outside of sports games too. Oliver worked on a lot of community projects, mostly ones that helped young people and sports programs for kids who don't have much. He supports the Munich street-soccer league Bunt kickt gut, which is considered a pioneer project of organised street-soccer and a Germany and Europe-wide model of intercultural understanding, education values and prevention; the Sepp-Herberger foundation, which promotes soccer in schools, clubs, and prisons; and the Justin Rockola Association, whose goal is the protection of young people against violence, alcohol and drugs.

When Oliver got to the top of his field, he never forgot the boost of support that helped him get there. His family, his teachers, and the muddy fields of Karlsruhe were always there for him. Oliver often went back to his roots out of gratitude, where he inspired the next generation of soccer fans with his appearance and words of support.

Of course, Oliver's journey had its share of problems and challenges, but his spirit never broke. Oliver reached the top of his career leading Germany to the World Cup final in 2002 and helping his country to get a third place on the World Cup in 2006. It's hard to describe how happy everyone in Karlsruhe was. Oliver's excellent play made him famous as one of the best keepers in World Cup history and a role model to follow by his fans all over the world.

After that, kids all over the world looked up to Oliver Kahn, the goalkeeper whose heart was as strong as the Rhine. From the muddy fields to the big arenas, his journey showed how important it is to keep going, work hard, and stay true to your roots. Oliver's life showed young people that if they worked hard at their dreams, no matter how strange they seemed, they could come true.

THE VAR

VAR, which stands for "Video Assistant Referee," was officially added to soccer to help referees make the right calls during games. VAR has been used in different ways by different soccer leagues and groups, but it became very well known on a global level.

In March 2018, VAR was given the green light by the International Football Association Board (IFAB), which is in charge of the rules of the game. Since then, more and more soccer leagues around the world have started to use it.

Here's a brief overview of the function and purpose of VAR:

Reviewing Key Decisions:

VAR is mostly used to look over four types of situations that can change the outcome of a game: goals, penalty decisions, straight red card incidents, and cases of mistaken identity where a red or yellow card was given to the wrong person.

On-Field Referee Assistance:

The referee on the field can ask the VAR team to look into certain incidents and give details. The VAR team can also suggest that the on-field judge do a review.

Clear and Obvious Errors:

It is the job of VAR to step in only when there is a clear mistake in the way decisions are made on the field. To make sure they get a full picture, the VAR team looks at the play from several camera views.

Maintaining the Flow of the Game:

The goal is to keep the flow of the game as smooth as possible. Decisions made by VAR are made quickly, and the referee on the field has the final say on whether to accept or change the ruling.

Communication Protocol:

Headsets make it easier for the on-field judge and the VAR team to talk to each other, which makes the decision-making process more coordinated and quicker.

Ensuring Fairness and Accuracy:

The goal of adding VAR is to make refereeing decisions fairer and more accurate, making it less likely that big mistakes will happen that change the result of a match.

It's important to remember that VAR isn't used the same way everywhere. It's been widely used in top leagues and foreign competitions, but not all soccer associations or leagues have adopted it. VAR may also be used in slightly different ways and in slightly different situations based on the competition and how the rules of the game are interpreted by the organizers.

Goalkeeper in action

CONCLUSION

Embracing the Goalkeeper's Legacy

The goalkeeper is a role model in the exciting world of soccer, where every goal tells a story and every save sounds like a victory. As the final whistle blows on this journey into the lives of goalkeeping stars, it's time to piece together the lessons, dreams, and strength that run through their stories. Being a goalkeeper isn't just about stopping shots; it's also about showing how people can keep going even when things get tough. Let's embark on a final kick into the goalmouth of inspiration, where the qualities needed to be the best soccer goalkeeper meet with the essence of chasing dreams in life.

What Dreams Are Made Of

And as I mentioned before just picture yourself in front of the goalposts with the stadium roaring with excitement, and the ball shooting straight at you. This is the heartbeat of dreams, the beat that runs through the life of a goalkeeper and the hopes and dreams of young people. How do you become the best soccer goalkeeper? To go beyond the limits of the field, you need a heart that beats with love, determination, and the guts to dream big.

The Chorus of Efforts Every great save is the result of a symphony of hard work that includes countless hours of practice, sacrifices, and a commitment to being the best.

The goalkeeper's journey isn't something they do alone; they work with their partners, coaches, and the memories of great players who have come before. When young dreamers step onto their own metaphorical fields, they need to know that to be great, they need to put in a lot of disciplined hard work and never give up on their dreams.

Making sacrifices and dream money

In the big stage of life, giving up things for your dreams becomes valuable. They missed gatherings, skipped social media time, social events and untold renunciations, paint a portrait of dedication that extends beyond the soccer field, goalkeepers show how dedicated they are in areas other than soccer. As young people set their sights on the stars, they should know that following their dreams often requires time, attention, and a willingness to put devotion as well as make big sacrifices. Every party you miss and practice hour you put in is like putting money into the bank of dreams. This money is called success, your future.

There were problems with the dance

It's not easy for a goalkeeper to get where they want to go; their journey is more like a dance with problems and struggles, a tango with setbacks, and a waltz with challenges. The goalkeeper's story isn't about the goals they stopped, but about the losses they faced and the lessons they learned. In the same way, life is a dance with problems. As young dreamers' pirouette through life's hurdles, they need to see problems and struggles as partners in the big dance of success. It's not about skipping steps; it's about mastering the dance.

The Dream Painting

Every goal, every save, and every moment of victory turns the soccer field into a painting where dreams come true. Just as each save the goalkeeper makes is a work of art, young dreamers have the power to paint their own canvases with aspirations, ambitions, and the vivid colors of their dreams and imagination. With its constantly shifting background, sports provide a unique opportunity for young people to express themselves, learn values, and write their own success stories.

Role models: lights to follow

In the maze of dreams, role models emerge as guiding lights illuminating the path to greatness. There are stories of goalkeepers who walked this path, people who stood tall between the posts and in life. Young people with big dreams need to know how important it is to have role models—not as impossible-to-reach idols, but as sources of inspiration. Legends are not born, they are made by people who work hard, persevere, and strive for greatness. Young readers and enthusiasts who are trying to find their way through the maze of their own dreams can use the stories of goalkeeping stars as compass points and guideposts.

Putting Values Together

The soccer field isn't just a place to play matches; it's a symphony where values like discipline, teamwork, resilience, and perseverance are played out with every kick of the ball. As young dreamers put on their "boots," they need to be aware of the symphony of values that is playing in the background. Sports can be used as a classroom to teach and learn important life lessons. This isn't just about getting goals; it's also about building character by being honest, respectful, and good sports.

Discipline: Which Makes You Who You Are

Having discipline is like having a leader for your character. It guides your dreams to the shores of success. When a goalkeeper with the discipline to improve skills, endure tough training, and stay focused during every game, they become a living example of this ability. Young people who want to reach their goals need to know that discipline is not a strict set of rules, but a way to find their way. To become great, you have to get up early to practice, study hard, and stay true to the commitments you have.

Being strong: The shield of dreams

Being tough helps the goalkeeper keep their dreams alive when they lose or have a loss. It's not a loss when you miss a save or let a goal in; it's a step toward getting better. In the face of defeats and setbacks, resilience becomes the shield that guards the dreams. Life also requires toughness, a shield that keeps goals safe from the arrows of doubt and failure. Young people with big dreams should see resilience as a talent that can turn problems into chances to grow and excel.

Perseverance: The Marathon of Dreams

Never giving up is like running a marathon of dreams, a race that goes beyond the soccer field. Goalkeepers are great examples of perseverance because they are always trying to get better. Before they start their journey through life, young people with big dreams need to know that success takes a long time. After going through the ups and downs, the turns and the twists, they should feel proud that they gave their best and cross the finish line.

Hearing the Sounds of Greatness

As the final whistle blows across the soccer field, the sounds of success can still be heard: a symphony of hard work, sacrifice, hardship, and victory. Young dreamers, as they absorb the stories of goalkeeping heroes should recognize that the qualities needed to be the best goalkeeper in soccer are the same qualities that make people great in life. The soccer field is more than just a place to play. It's also a training ground for life's grand game where kids can learn how to play the big game of life and where each youngster has the potential to become the guardian of their dreams.

Who Keeps Dreams Safe

In conclusion, the goalkeeper isn't just the guardian of the goal; they're also the guardian of dreams. A goalkeeper's journey is not a solitary odyssey, but a collective story that includes the stories of those who came before and those who will come after. Young dreams, chase your dreams they are there for you!

Disclaimer

This book is written with young readers in mind and it hopes to motivate and inspire them to pursue their dreams and aspirations, work hard in life and overcome struggles. Any decisions or actions taken in reliance on the information contained in this book are not the author's responsibility.

Thank you for choosing us, we value your Amazon review immensely. Your thoughts and feedback are highly appreciated. Thank you for taking the time to share!

ISBN: 9798871861028

Copyright © 2023 by Kurt Dissel
All rights reserved

Printed in Great Britain
by Amazon